Beyond the Mountains:
Overcoming the Challenges Within
10 Lessons for Leading in Crisis

Beyond the Mountains:
Overcoming the Challenges Within
10 Lessons for Leading in Crisis

Pangi Valley

Photo credit: Ashok Dilwali

Sunder Hemrajani

Allied Publishers Pvt. Ltd.
NEW DELHI • MUMBAI • KOLKATA
CHENNAI • BANGALORE • HYDERABAD

ALLIED PUBLISHERS PRIVATE LIMITED

1/13-14 Asaf Ali Road, **New Delhi**–110002
Ph.: 011-23239001 • E-mail: delhi.books@alliedpublishers.com

17 Chittaranjan Avenue, **Kolkata**–700072
Ph.: 033-22129618 • E-mail: cal.books@alliedpublishers.com

15 J.N. Heredia Marg, Ballard Estate, **Mumbai**–400001
Ph.: 022-42126969 • E-mail: mumbai.books@alliedpublishers.com

No. 25/10 Commander-in-Chief Road, Ethiraj Lane (Next to Post Office) Egmore, **Chennai**–600008
Ph.: 044-28223938 • E-mail: chennai.books@alliedpublishers.com

P.B No. 9932, No. 15, 3rd Floor (Next to Vijaya Bank), 5th Cross, Gandhinagar, Karnataka, **Bangalore**–560009
Ph.: 080-41530285 / 22386239
• E-mail: bngl.journals@alliedpublishers.com / apsabng@airtelmail.in

Sri Jayalakshmi Nilayam, No. 3-4-510, 3rd Floor (Above More Super Market) Barkatpura, **Hyderabad**–500027
Ph.: 040-27551811, 040-27551812 • E-mail: hyd.books@alliedpublishers.com

Website: www.alliedpublishers.com

© 2021, Author

No part of the material protected by this copyright notice may be reproduced or utilized in any form or by any means, electronic or mechanical including photocopying, recording or by any information storage and retrieval system, without prior written permission from the copyright owners.

ISBN: 978-93-89934-27-4

Brahma Peak

Brahma Peak is located in the Kishtwar range of Himalayas in South of Kashmir. It is the third highest peak, but the most prominent and attractive in the range. There had been several attempts on Brahma, some of them resulting in fatalities till it was first climbed by the famous British mountaineer Chris Bonington and Nick Estcourt in 1973. Chris called Kishtwar range the 'true mountain playground for future generations'.

Dedicated to

the

Red Building of Dreams

Foreword

"Two roads diverged in a wood, and I . . . I took the one less travelled by, and that has made all the difference."
—American poet Robert Frost

In 1976, we at the Faculty of Management Studies (FMS), University of Delhi *took the less travelled road* and were the first business school in India to organize a Trekking Club. The idea of organizing a Trekking Club at FMS was inspired by my curiosity when I read about the use of flight simulators to train trainee pilots enrolled in the aviation schools. The flight simulators have been used for training trainee pilots 'on ground' before sending them off for airborne missions. I found close parallels between a business school and an aviation school—the former trained leaders to run business enterprises and latter trained the pilots to run flying machines. It made lot of sense to me and a handful of students at FMS to organize a 'leadership simulator' as an extension of the education at FMS. So, equipped with a half-baked logic of creating a leadership simulator, we approached Professor S. Neelamegham, the then Dean of FMS to help us in initiating the Trekking Club at FMS. He was quick and understood the importance of organising trekking expeditions as a means to giving experience in leadership, teamwork and most importantly risk taking to young students. Thus, the idea of a trekking club at FMS was born and 'officialised'.

Indeed, there is one big difference in a flight simulator and a trekking expedition as a leadership simulator. The flight simulator is a static machine and works based on algorithms, equations, control instruments and virtually created visuals... in your final test on a flight simulator if you crash you make big thumping noise and you are still sitting in the seat waiting for the flight instructor to mark you 'failed'. On the other hand, a trekking expedition as a leadership simulator presents real contexts, real risks and real experiences... and it is these real experiences which prepare young business students to learn lessons in conceiving, organising, launching and leading missions in high risk environments.

Organising and mounting a high-altitude trekking expedition in Himalayas is no less than leading and managing a business enterprise in a high-risk environment. In Himalayas, like any other snow-covered mountain ranges, the inherent risks in the form of inclement weather or boulders rolling off the cliffs or snow avalanches moving at enormous sweeping speeds are actually worse than the nature of risk leaders face in business situations. It is the element of surprise, magnitude and speed at which the risks happen on the mountains that can make a difference and, in few seconds, instil shock and fear or at worst inflict fatalities.

We had to do immense preparations before launching our trekking expeditions to unfamiliar terrains with no life support services in place. We did not know enough about principles of risk taking on mountains except limited experience some of us had of participating in trekking programmes arranged by the Youth Hostel Association of India (YHAI). Our decisions and plans were based on rudimentary information and a 'packing list' given to us by YHAI. Then thirty years later, my friend and colleague at Oxford, Pete Goss, a British yachtsman explained the meaning of adventure and risk taking. He said, "successful adventure leaders don't take risk, they 'embrace' risk and prepare and train for every possible scenario. You run and rerun riskiest of the situations in your mind and prepare. As a leader you can't be so irresponsible that you push your team members into unknown situations and unprepared." Pete's words made lot of sense and I learnt how to 'master' risk rather than 'take' risk!

To comply with the long 'packing list' we had to make huge preparations to 'embrace risk' on the mountains. It basically meant that we needed finances to arrange equipment, shoes, thermal clothing, medicines, food, cooking stoves and kerosene. The financial support from FMS was limited and we were given a small budget just enough to cover our travel costs to base station and accommodation in forest rest houses or Public Works Department bungalows or night shelters in jungles 'prepared' by nomads.

Undeterred by the fact that we had loads of uncovered expenses, we started to tap our alumni in pharma and food and beverages companies in New Delhi. My brother-in-law Professor Harish Saxena, the then President of Youth Hostel Association of India was most gracious in lending equipment and personal gear for our team members. I would like to express my gratitude to all sponsors who made it possible to take this expedition forward.

To manage our budget, we decided to take the responsibility of carrying the loads ourselves. We ensured that we had some members in the expedition who could cook, give first aid and entertain when sprits were down! We carried rations, medicines and kerosene for the entire duration of the trek.

This was an important lesson—lack of resources should not discourage a leader and the team from pursuing the mission. You need to go out and tap into your network of friends and alumni to raise resources. There is always someone around you who will appreciate the purpose of your passion and mission and support you in your endeavour. All you need is a compelling story to tell the people to arouse their interest and support for your mission. You need to discover essential skills within the team. You need to learn continuously—on the first day the food may not taste good, keep trying and you will improve with each passing day!

Throughout the history of trekking expeditions by FMS students, we were able to raise adequate material resources by tapping into our connections in our professional circles and the corporate world at large. In the latter years, the trekkers alumni themselves became the big supporters of the trekking expeditions at FMS and came forward to support an underfunded adventure activity. The Trekking Club at FMS has been an outstanding success!

A trekking expedition from A to is essentially *team collaboration, teamwork, team enthusiasm, team energy and team commitment*. Every member of the expedition is tested physically, mentally, emotionally, and even spiritually and as we had our very dear fellow students from other countries join the expeditions, we were tested cross-culturally. We discovered another important lesson that when we created a mutually supportive seamless shared experience, we could address the stresses of individuals. A word of empathy to one who is thinking of quitting, a hand of support to carry extra load, offering a cup of hot soup to the tired or giving a pill to mitigate pain might sound little gestures but they go a long way in restoring the group energy and enthusiasm to reach the destination.

Foreword

On trekking expeditions we discovered that the team energy and enthusiasm followed a sine curve—sometimes up sometimes down. We learnt the importance of observing, listening and using the sixth sense to feel how individual members are feeling and act instantly in restoring their self-belief and confidence. Participating in an extended adventure expedition gives a kind of crucible experience—the negativity evaporates and the best comes out!

This book by my student and friend Sunder Hemrajani is a beautiful account of two FMS expeditions. He led one of the two expeditions. He has chronicled the day to day events and has extracted some profound lessons in leadership.

Sunder is a wise man! Instead of rushing to write a quick book, he discussed and tested his reflections on his trekking experiences with young students in the business school by organizing workshops. He met professionals in publishing industry to develop an inspiring text for this book. He tested these lessons in his professional journey as a corporate business leader as well as in his personal life. In the end, we have a fine text on leadership based on his first hand experiences.

My best wishes to Sunder, all the former trekkers at FMS, our sponsors and FMS colleagues. It has been a fascinating experience to reflect on why and how we pioneered a "leadership simulator" in a business school.

Lalit Johri
Founder Chair, Transformation Paradigms
Senior Fellow in International Business,
University of Oxford (2007-19)

Acknowledgements

The Faculty of Management Studies (FMS), University of Delhi is one of the leading institutions in the field of management education in India. It started with a modest beginning in 1954 and in the past 65 years it has witnessed significant growth and development. Apart from the classroom education, it puts the students through leadership experiences by giving the opportunities to participate in various academic and non-academic activities.

There were several activities managed by the students like convention, placement, cultural and sports. While these were not a part of the academic curriculum, these experiences helped the students to hone their soft skills. I learnt valuable lessons in leadership and teamwork on the playing fields and the treks, not inside the classroom. I must add that these experiences helped me in navigating challenges in corporate and personal life later on.

At the outset, I must acknowledge the contribution of Dr. Lalit Johri to this effort. His pioneering initiative at FMS put trekking on the FMS calendar. Lalit also helped me with this book. He went through the first draft and gave me invaluable suggestions. He has been an inspiration and a guide. He has also written the foreword.

Credit is also due to Kapil Malhotra, a senior Modernite and a reputed publisher who gave me professional advice on this project. The students who engaged with me during the workshops on the subject at FMS also provided me with some very good insights.

While lockdown has had some downsides, it has given me an opportunity to enhance my learning through attending webinars on the Covid situation conducted especially by the faculty of my alma mater, Harvard Business School (HBS) where I attended the Advanced Management Program (AMP) in 2011. Leadership during the crisis has been an underlying theme of these webinars. I would like to mention that over the last few years, I have attended several sessions on leadership conducted by my friend and a fellow Modernite Prof. Ranjay Gulati of HBS. I have leveraged these learnings for this book.

I must express my gratitude to my Modern School classmate and childhood friend Ravi Sachdev and his able editorial chief Sharad Gupta who helped me with good advice for bringing out this book.

Finally, I would like to thank my wonderful wife Kamala who had to bear with my unending hours on laptop to write the book during the lockdown and my sons Akhil and Rohan who were working from home in Manila and Minneapolis, for their inputs.

Preface

Every event in life has a context. We are encouraged to take decisions based on the context and the options which present themselves. Right from my school days, I had taken keen interest in trekking and mountaineering. At various stages of my life, I availed of the opportunity to go for treks, attended rock climbing program at Nuh organised by Delhi Mountaineering Association and also enrolled for the Basic Mountaineering Course at Himalayan Mountaineering Institute at Darjeeling in 1983. I couldn't finish the course because of sickness. My love for mountains started with the school trips at my alma mater Modern School where I got exposed to trekking in and around Nainital and Dalhousie (Khajjiar, Chamba).

Sunder rappelling down the Tenzing Rock in Darjeeling

Passion for the mountains has been a constant theme of my personal life. So, when the opportunity of the Expedition 2 to Margan Pass (13000 ft) presented itself, I had no hesitation in joining along with 10 other students from 1st and 2nd years of the MBA program at FMS, University of Delhi. This was a milestone for me. I subsequently led the Expedition 3 to Sach Pass (15000 ft). The learnings from these real-life events were life changing. The lessons learnt were to shape my corporate career which was to follow after the MBA Program.

During the expeditions, you go through real life experiences which help you to test and improve your leadership skills. The expeditions were like a leadership laboratory on teamwork, risk taking, project strategizing, resourcing, planning, inter-personal conflict resolution and crisis management. Needless to say, at a personal level, it was a humbling experience.

I have shared these experiences with various generations of students at FMS in the form of a case study, hoping that someday they would benefit from these lessons. I could have written this book earlier in my life but I would have perhaps missed out on the leadership experiences and formal leadership concepts which I have learnt along the way.

There are various genres of books on 'Leadership'. I have personally read quite a few in my life. I was fortunate to attend leadership programs in Hindustan Unilever, Whirlpool and PepsiCo where I got exposed to various concepts on leadership. Most books authored by academics are based on the research work done by them. There are others penned by respected and successful corporate leaders based on their experiences. I was keen to bring out a book which was light reading targeted at younger generation of students and executives at the beginning of their career journey. Something which they could read in 1-2 sessions and read it multiple times as they progressed in their life. Hence I adopted a simple storytelling style.

I started working on the book in 2017. I conducted 2 workshops at FMS for the MBA classes of 2019 and 2020 to get some insights regarding the challenges faced by the current generation of students. I also encouraged them to share their thoughts on some of the challenges faced by the teams and the key issues addressed by them on these treks.

The FMS Trekking era started sometime in 1976 with FMS Expedition 1. This was largely as a result of the initiative taken by Dr. Lalit Johri who apart from teaching Marketing subjects in the classroom was a trekker of merit. The idea of FMS Trekking Expeditions was a culmination of the desire for adventure amongst the students and Dr Johri's passion for trekking. He was the force behind this initiative at FMS. He planned and led the FMS Expedition I in 1976 and FMS Expedition 2 in 1977.

The thought behind this initiative was to facilitate bonding between students of both the batches (1st and 2nd year) and promote the spirit of adventure amongst them. The treks tested the fitness—physical and mental of the trekkers because the groups faced uncertain conditions and had to find solutions in unfamiliar surroundings, a scenario not alien in the modern world of management. There were many other leadership and management lessons learnt on the treks. The era ended sometime in 90s with the departure of Dr Johri who left FMS to pursue his dreams overseas.

I was a member of FMS Expedition 2 (Margan Pass, 13000 ft) and Leader of FMS Expedition 3 (Sach Pass, 15000 ft) and have put together my perspective on this unique and exciting initiative.

> *"You are what your deepest desire is.*
> *As your desire is, so is your intention.*
> *As your intention is, so is your will.*
> *As your will is, so is your deed.*
> *As your deed is, so is your destiny."*
>
> Brihadaranyaka Upanishad

Contents

Foreword 7
Acknowledgements 13
Preface 15

1. FMS Expedition 2 21
2. Interlude 37
3. FMS Expedition 3 43
4. Expedition 2 and 3: Life Lessons Learnt 67
5. Life Lesson 1: Articulating a Compelling Vision 68
   that Inspires Others to Follow
6. Life Lesson 2: Take Appropriate, ... 71
   Well-Reasoned Risks
7. Life Lesson 3: Foster Trust and Bounded 73
   Optimism in Crisis
8. Life Lesson 4: Teamwork is a Force Multiplier 75
9. Life Lesson 5: Demonstrate Perseverance and 77
   Resilience in Pursuit of Goals
10. Life Lesson 6: Empathy is an Important Virtue 79
11. Life Lesson 7: Self-Confidence is Contagious 81
12. Life Lesson 8: Encourage the Heart and 83
    Celebrate Success
13. Life Lesson 9: Confront and Resolve Tough Issues 85
14. Life Lesson 10: Play to Win 88
15. The Big Lessons for Life 90

Bibliography 93

FMS Expedition 2

FMS Expedition 2 to Margan Pass set out for Jammu on a train on the last day of September 1977. Margan Pass is a mountain pass, connecting Warwan Valley with the main Kashmir Valley. It is situated 35 km from Kokernag, a sub-district town in Breng Valley, Anantnag district known for its gardens, pristine fresh-water springs and rainbow trout farms. The pass, also referred as Margan Top, perched at a height of approx. 13000 ft is a gateway to the hidden Warwan Valley in Kishtwar district. The name is derived from the words 'Mar' which means death and 'Gan' which connotes a valley. It's known for its unpredictable weather and hence called the valley of death. In the olden days, there used to be death and destruction of trekkers, travellers and livestock due to snowstorms and blizzards.

The area is also known for its grassy meadows. The Gujjar and Bakerwal tribesmen bring their livestock—goats and sheep for grazing for a few months.

The plan was to use the autumn vacation for the trek to avoid missing the academic classes. The prior four weeks were spent planning the details including the route, train tickets, equipment and all other logistics details. Lalit who had considerable experience leveraged his contacts in the Youth Hostel Association to work out the details. When the risk is embraced, the importance of advance planning and preparation cannot be understated. The dividing line between success and failure is very thin.

The 11 member team consisted of 4 students from the 2nd year, Ahmed Ayyash (Deputy Leader), Kamal Oberoi,

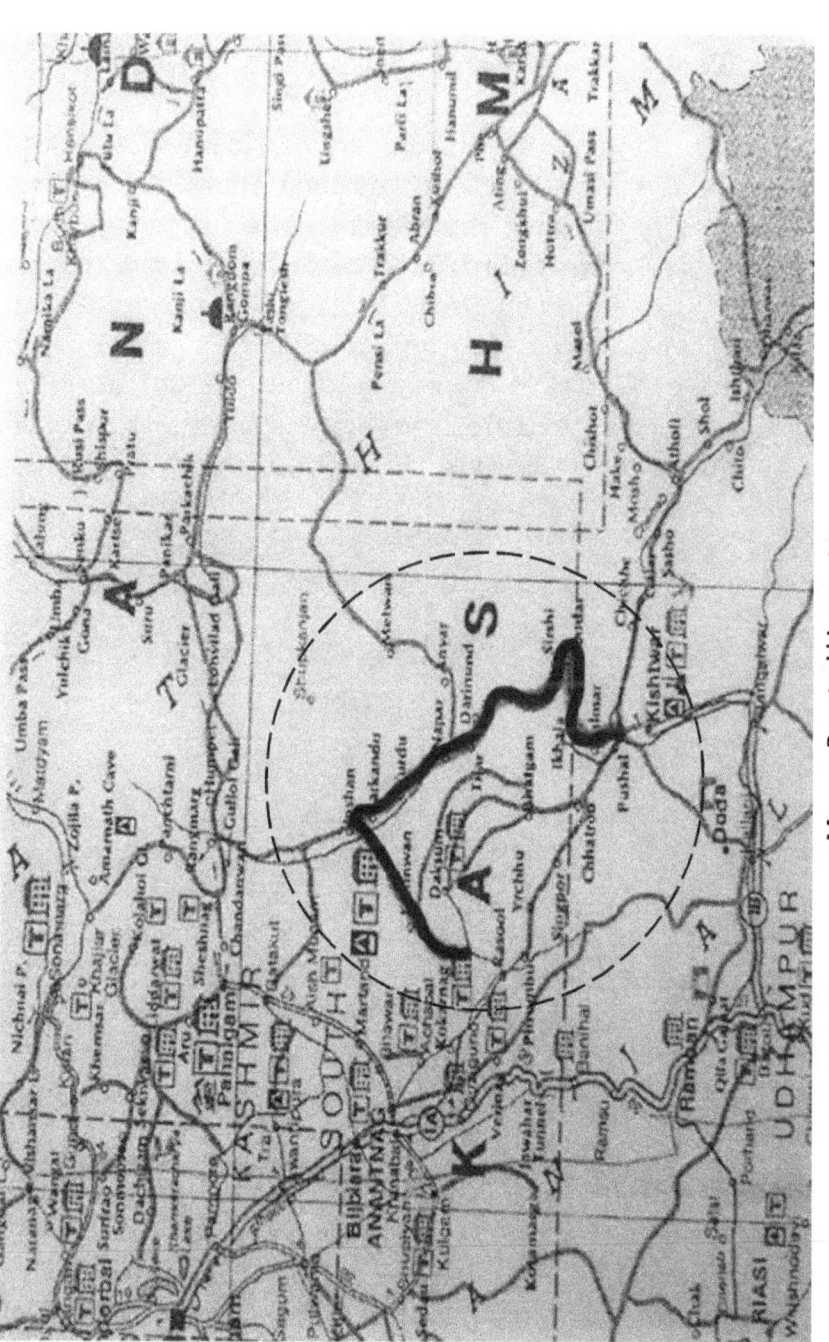

Margan Pass trekking route

Chandrasekhar and Navin Sagar. Sandeep Kohli, Rahul Yadav, SV Krishnan (Krish), NK Gupta (NK), Dalip Raheja and I constituted the 1st year group. Dr Lalit Johri (Lalit) was the Leader of the team. All members carried a rucksack to accommodate personal effects and their share of the group resources like the medicines, jerry cans for fuel, stoves, provisions for food and not to forget bottles of Viva and Maltova donated by expedition sponsors. This dose of energy provided by these products on long stretches and in the morning before the day's trek was extremely valuable for the tired trekkers. The fuel and fresh vegetables were to be picked up from the base at Kishtwar in Jammu region.

Maltova break for the extra energy

There was nothing notable in the train journey to Jammu. Some members had also smuggled in bottles of rum ostensibly to counter the low temperatures at the heights. However, the consumption started on the plains as the train chugged out of the Delhi railway station. This was to have consequences later.

The transit halt at Jammu was to unwind and facilitate bonding amongst the team. It also enabled us to get used to dormitory living at Jammu Bus Station from where we took a bus to Kishtwar via Doda. Kishtwar is a municipality in Kishtwar district of Jammu region and is located 235 km from Jammu. The bus journey commenced on the Jammu-Srinagar highway. We had lunch consisting of Rajma-Chawal at Batote and resumed our journey. From there we took a turn to Doda and Kishtwar. The road was treacherous but scenic. The Chenab river kept our company till Doda where we had a brief stopover for Pakoda and Chai. We reached the destination Kishtwar, a district headquarter town in the evening and ensconced ourselves in the Inspection Bungalow. This was an important break to ensure the team acclimatised to the altitude. We spent the next 2 days going up and down the surrounding hills with rucksacks on our backs. We also picked up fresh vegetables and kerosene from the local bazar. Evenings were for relaxation. The 2 days at the base were extremely useful for preparing the team for a tough trek ahead.

Day 1 of the trek started with an early breakfast followed by a 90 minute bus ride to Palmar, the last bus-head from where we started trekking. Everyone was given packed lunch—Puri and Aloo Subzi prepared by the unofficial cook NK. This was to become staple diet during the trek. It was expected to be a long day. It was a 11 km trek to Ikhala. With approx. 18 kgs on the back, the team made slow progress. The advance group sat down for lunch near the trail. It got tougher as the day went by. The body was not yet used to the heavy weight we were all carrying. On the way, we walked through green meadows where the local tribesmen

Striding towards the destination on Day 1

Short lunch break on the trail on Day 1, somewhere between Palmar and Ikhala

and women were busy looking after their livestock grazing on the meadows. After some time, the group broke up into 3-4 smaller sub-groups depending on the pace. Lalit being the leader of the group stayed with the stragglers. I was a part of the first group which reached Ikhala after a few rest breaks, in the evening. It was followed by a long wait for others. It was becoming dark and the last group had still not made it. I along with other members took out our torches and went looking for team-mates and the leader. It was a long walk before we came across the group. Some members were struggling. Dalip was quite sick. We helped them with their rucksacks and brought them to Ikhala. NK had prepared Dal-Rice for dinner. Dalip was given some medicine to recover since next day the team had to start in the morning for the next leg. Dalip's condition was worrying and the decision on him was postponed to next morning.

Navin was ready with cups of hot tea early morning. It was time to get ready, prepare breakfast and packed lunch for Day 2, 11 km trek to Sounder. Lalit was not very happy with Dalip's condition which had not improved. He had not eaten anything and was clearly sick and unfit to proceed. Lalit took the difficult decision to take him back to a lower altitude to Palmar and put him on the bus back to Kishtwar so that he could head back to Delhi. He asked me to accompany him and instructed the group to stay at Ikhala till we returned.

The journey to Palmar was difficult. Dalip was in no position to walk back. We decided to halt at a mid-point at a dhaba. The closest doctor was at Palmar. Lalit asked me to go to Palmar to consult the doctor and get medicine while he and Dalip waited at the dhaba. It was quite dark by the time I returned. Dalip's condition improved after taking medicine and night rest. Lalit hired the mule next day for him and both he and I escorted him to Palmar. The daily bus had just

Trudging back to Palmar with Dalip

arrived. We were quite relieved to send him to Kishtwar. There was no way he could have continued on the trek. It was a lesson for the team. It's important to respect the environment. Complacency can lead to serious consequences.

Lalit and I trekked back to Ikhala to join the group who were eagerly waiting for us. Next morning, the team left for Sounder. The teamwork in the group was amazing. The adversity had brought the group together.

The trek to Sounder was uneventful. Here, for the first time we got the glimpse of the magnificent Brahma Peak known for the difficult climb. The trail passed through heavily forested gorges. We reached the destination in different groups well before dark and stayed in a farm cottage surrounded by dried farm produce. The next day's trek to Sirshi was short. It gave us enough time to rest and take a refreshing shower in a waterfall. Fortunately, everyone was

Resting time near a waterfall

coping with the trek pretty well. Minor ailments were dealt with by our own medicine man Krish who administered vitamins and medicine with an expertise of a doctor.

Time to rehydrate

A break to rest

The group left for the next stage to Hanzal next morning after the usual tea and breakfast. We walked through rich farmland and also got a spectacular view of Brahma Peak. Yourdu was the next halt. By now, the boys were speeding up. The body had now got acclimatised to the environment. As we approached Yourdu, we came across apple and walnut orchards. The team was getting closer to the ultimate goal. The mood in the group was quite upbeat. The members were now enjoying the roles assigned to them. Yourdu to Inshan was a beautiful landscape, along river Warwan. We reached there early thereby getting some time to rest and unwind. Some of the boys were complaining about aches and pains. The problems got 'accentuated' since a pretty lady doctor was in attendance in the village.

Next day was the big day since there was a long 16 km distance to be covered to cross Margan Pass into Lahinwan.

The team on the dry riverbed near the Margan Pass

FMS Expedition 2 31

Enroute to Margan Pass

We decided to start early so the boys were up at 4 am and ready for the grind at 5 am. Lalit was a leader who led

Successful team on the rocky terrain of Margan Pass

from the front. I brought up the rear. The group had to stay together. The objective was to reach bus-head in Lahinwan to catch the last bus to Kokernag. The trekkers made good progress and left the tree line behind to walk into a rocky barren area. Margan Pass is a crossover point from Jammu region into Kashmir region. The team encountered number of mules carrying provision from Lahinwan into the other side. We had not seen any vehicle since getting off the bus at Palmar. When we reached Lahinwan in late afternoon, the boys did a big hurrah and went and hugged a jeep.

The expedition had been successful. To celebrate it, the group had a hot cup of tea at a dhaba followed by sumptuous Aloo Parathas at Kokernag. All the participants had lost weight after a strenuous trek. The next day, before leaving for Srinagar, the team had a shower and good breakfast. The final celebration was kept for Srinagar where we had an

Celebrating success in Kokernag—Lalit with the team, Navin, Rahul, NK, Sandeep, Chandra, Kamal, Ahmed, Sunder, Krish

evening of wild dancing and fun. The team returned to Delhi the next day after a tiring journey to much jubilation at FMS.

It was important to narrate the story of Expedition 2 since it set the stage for what was to follow in the next adventure. The lessons were quite clear. It's important to respect the environment on such missions. Teamwork is absolutely critical for such expeditions to succeed. Every member moved into a role depending on capability.

Besides displaying their skill and determination in trekking, the boys showed their class in other fields—from cooking food to mending clothes. Here are the profile of the trekkers.

Dr Lalit Johri, the leader of the expedition proved himself in that capacity by making very timely and appropriate decisions. Apart from being an experienced trekker, he distinguished himself in the kitchen specialising in soup and juice preparations. Fortunately for the expedition members, he didn't live up to his 'no-nonsense' image and made the trek very enjoyable by his gimmicks. Who would forget that evening in Srinagar!

Ahmed Ayyash, the Deputy Leader and a very colourful personality was a prominent member of the 'Kitchen' group and enjoyed a monopoly in preparation of Rice, Tea and above all Maltova. He displayed tremendous courage on the trek and had the distinction of killing a poisonous snake enroute. It is reported that in Ahmed's chance encounter with a ferocious animal, the animal ran away howling with fear ('The animal is frightened' to quote Ahmed). The description won't be complete without the mention of 'Ikhala Affair'.

Navin Sagar started the trek on an uncertain note but later pulled through very well. An early riser, he used to wake up the rest of the members but had to discontinue this practice after encountering hostile reaction from the members. Poor chap, once got muscle cramps after eating (perfectly hygienic) 'Paranthas' in Sounder, thereby opening new territories for medicinal research.

Chandrasekhar (Chandra) made his reputation on the trek as a 'Darner'. In the evening, one could see him mending clothes of the members. Sometimes the members used to wonder what this bright talented young boy was doing in FMS. Burlingtons would be a better proposition. As far as trekking is concerned, he was a firm believer in 'slow and steady' principle.

Kamal Oberoi, the unofficial 'Cook', sorry 'Chef' of the trek, scaled great heights in preparation of Dal and frying of Puris. Certainly an asset to his family. His bottle dance—a la Garba, in Inshan brought forth the hidden talent.

Rahul Yadav, a jovial personality was a fine entertainer when 'in mood' and had the ability of running Keshto Mukherji out of business. Some of his acts led to call for a repeat performance. Rahul was a strong favourite with bugs. He proved to be a tough trekker.

Sandeep Kohli, 'a man with a kerosene oil tin' (a worthy substitute for the Golden Gun) was another tough man of the trek. His *'Kahan Laake Maara Re'* chant became very popular with the tired trekkers on tough stretches. As a leader of the Bhangra group of Afghanistan, he did full justice to his role.

NK Gupta (NK) rolling puris with an empty bottle was a familiar sight on the trek. There was a proposal by the members to me (Placement Secretary) to arrange summer internship for NK in Kake-Da-Hotal. The idea was given serious consideration. He was indeed a fine trekker.

SV Krishnan, 'Krish' as he was popularly called, was the Medicine Man of the trek. Krish was a real asset to the expedition. His melodious songs were as stimulating as the Vitamin capsules which he used to distribute in the evenings.

I, Sunder Hemrajani was a member of rescue squad. I proved to be a dismal failure on the kitchen front and pledged to improve on that front before the next trek.

The list of personalities will not be complete without the mention of Atlas of the group—Dalip Raheja. Unfortunately, the 'earth' proved too heavy for him, retired hurt and went back to the pavilion. His exuberance was missed throughout the trip.

Mature leadership provided by Lalit made a huge difference. He took the difficult decision to send a member back for the greater good of the team. He got the little things right and created an environment of trust.

More importantly, I had established my credentials as a team player and a strong trekker. The rescue act in Ikhala also gave me the confidence that I could raise my performance when faced with adversity.

Interlude

The second academic year started in July with the first event on the calendar, MSA (Management Science Association) Elections. MSA was a body which represented all full time students at FMS. The students elected their representatives for the positions of General Secretary, Convention Secretary, Placement Secretary, Cultural Secretary and Treasurer. Unlike first year, this time a lot of heat was generated. The entire class of 45 students was split down the middle. It was extremely competitive. I was fortunate to get re-elected as Placement Secretary from our syndicate.

The next expedition was planned in the aftermath of bitterly fought election. The success of the previous expedition had led to increased interest and participation from the class. Twelve persons signed up: Sandeep, Krishnan, NK Gupta and I had been on the trek previous year. Raghuraman, Sunil, Shekar, Deepak, Hamid, Uday, Sanjay and Mallya (1st year) were the first timers. There was a surprise in store for us. Dr Lalit Johri, the most experienced trekker and designated leader for FMS Expedition 3 decided to get married around the same time. Hence I was nominated by him to lead the expedition. Suddenly I was pitch forked into the hot seat. Sandeep was the Deputy Leader.

Needless to say, like the previous expedition, the team's skills went beyond trekking. A team is a tapestry of individuals who bring different capabilities to the team. Like the FMS Expedition 2 previous year, the members of the team took on various responsibilities. There were some newcomers who were on their first trek and hence were spared the onerous jobs.

Hamid with his rugged looks

Hamidullah Helmandi (Hamid) was the strongman of the trek. He was from Afghanistan which has a mountainous and tough terrain. He took to the tough trek like fish to the water. He was always willing to carry a heavy load. I knew I could always rely on him in case of any crisis.

Shekar Swamy, 'Stretch' as he was fondly called was the quiet one. This was his first trek and he started slowly but finished it with a flourish. He would help with some errands in the evening like fetching water from the nearby stream for cooking. Otherwise, you could see him sitting in a corner recovering from the day's exertions.

Deepak Raj Bhandary, 'Brandy' was from Nepal and hence we assumed he would find the trek easy. But he realized that the ups and downs on the mule tracks in the mountains

Interlude

were very different from walking the streets of Kathmandu. He had a difficult first few days but managed quite well in the second half of the trek.

Uday Kumar, 'Buds' was a slow and steady trekker. He had a distinctive blue rucksack and hence you could recognize him from a distance. This was his first trek. He was very steady and was always smiling. You could barely sense that he was finding it tough especially during the first few days. He also finished well.

Sanjay Jain (Sanjay) kept a low profile during the first few days but came into his elements during the celebratory evening in Killar. He and Krish entertained us that evening. He enjoyed the trekking experience though I am not sure if he would have volunteered for another trek.

The team photo at Brindabani
Front (L to R): Krish, NK, Raghu, Sanjay, Shekar
Back (L to R): Uday, Sunder, Mallya, Brandy, Sandeep, Sunil.

Sunil Mangla (Sunil) had a great trek. Against all odds, he started the trek well and ended it on a high. From a distance he used to resemble a 'bouncing' rucksack. His 'bouncing stance' up and down the trail caused a problem on the way when the sleeping bag tied to his rucksack got detached and rolled down a valley on the way to Dharwas. We had to go down and fetch it.

Sunil and Sunder on the trail to Dharwas

Raghuraman (Raghu) did well on the trek. He had his close friends Krish and NK to inspire him along the way. He also provided able support to NK in the kitchen. He was always willing to help. Kept a low profile but showed strength when it mattered.

Krishnan (Krish) was once again the go to person for all ailments—sore ankles, blisters, muscular pain and headaches. He was the medicine man, a repeat of FMS Expedition 2. His jovial disposition and positive attitude was infectious.

Interlude 41

Raghu and Krish on the trail

His performance at Killar changed the mood on the trek. He made an awesome contribution.

NK Gupta was an important member of the team. Apart from trekking skills, the most important attribute on any expedition is the cooking skill. As the unofficial cook, NK had to manage with limited resources, a kerosene stove and limited implements. After a hard day's trek, he had to prepare dinner for the hungry trekkers and lunch for next day which was packed in plastic lunch boxes. He did a commendable job on the trek, notwithstanding the blowout situation in Sohol.

Vijay Mallya was the only one from the first year to join the trekking team. He was not as colorful as his industrialist namesake but made up with some nice color pictures on the trek. He was the only one to carry a camera with a color film. Must thank him for the color pics which the readers will see in this book.

NK enjoying the scenic landscape

Sandeep Kohli (Sandeep) was appointed Deputy Leader of the team. I knew I could always lean on him in case there was any crisis to handle. He was a very valuable support, a strong trekker and continued to motivate the team on difficult stretches.

I was thrust into the leadership role in early September once Lalit decided to withdraw from the trek due to his impending marriage to Meera, our senior at FMS. He made up by preparing me for the trek. His briefing about the route and each location was very accurate. He had an amazing memory. He was thorough especially on dos' and don'ts and set us up for success.

Next few weeks were spent preparing for the trek. Last year's experience and Lalit's presence helped immensely. He was present at FMS to see the team off. The destination was Sach Pass (15000 ft).

FMS Expedition 3

The train journey to Jammu and then a bus ride to Kishtwar was uneventful. The lessons from the previous year were imbibed by the team. Sach Pass at 15000 ft was a more difficult trek compared to Margan Pass. Sach Pass (15000 ft) is located in Chamba District in Himachal Pradesh. It offers the shortest route to district headquarter town of Killar, famous for its rich natural beauty. It is also a gateway to the picturesque Pangi Valley in the Pir Panjal range of Himalayas. The Pangi Valley is a remote, rugged and poorly developed tribal area. It is unique in its grandeur and beauty. The gushing Chandrabhaga river flows through the valley.

Water of life in the mountains

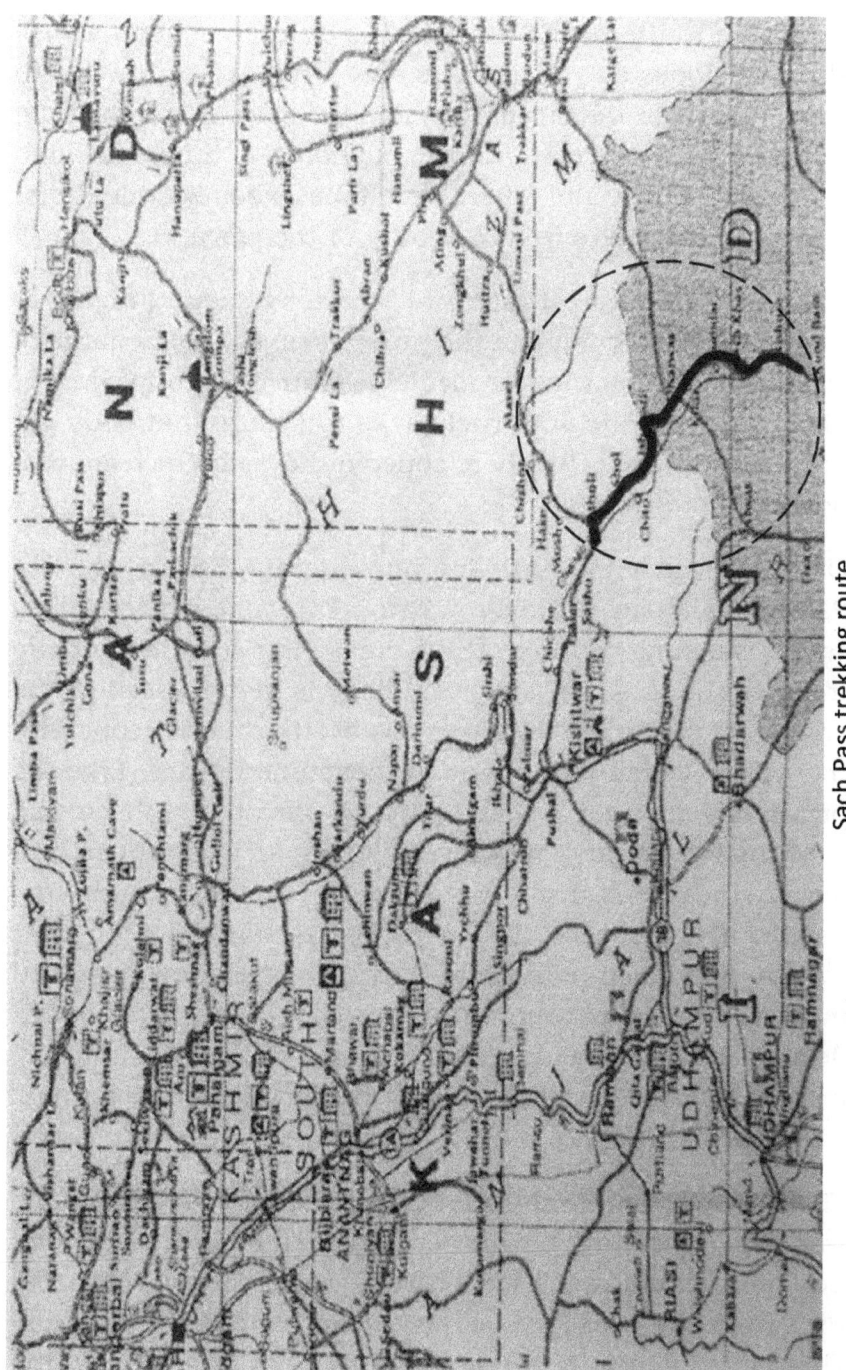

Sach Pass trekking route

The route to the pass from Killar is quite treacherous with slippery slopes and dangerous crevasses. It is advisable to cross it early in the morning before the snow starts melting. The area with fir trees with the backdrop of the mountains is incredibly beautiful. There were times when we would just take a break to admire the beauty of the place.

The base camp was at Kishtwar where we spent 2 nights to acclimatise and complete the purchases. NK took charge of cooking and Krish was our medicine man. The group climbed hills in the vicinity with rucksacks to ensure that body got used to the weight. Freshers coped quite well. The team was now ready to trek.

Day 1 started with a 90 mins bus ride to Atholi, a tehsil in Paddar Valley in Kishtwar district. Everyone carried rucksacks weighing approx. 18-20 kgs. First few days of the trek are the toughest since the body is getting used to the additional weight. As the days pass by, the muscles cope with the weight which reduces as we consume rations. Like the previous year, every member would offer the stuff he was carrying for the days cooking. Carrying fuel containers was tough since we had to carry them in hands. It couldn't be packed in a rucksack. The first day trek was quite tough. It was up and down right up to Sohol. The trekkers staggered into the forest department hut. The cooking team led by NK decided to get on with cooking dinner which was nothing more than Dal-Rice followed by Puris and Aloo Subzi for next day's packed lunch.

There were complaints about the difficult day. Everyone was eagerly waiting for dinner and then a good night rest. Suddenly, there was a loud hiss and everyone saw the Dal Rice from the pressure cooker escape and hit the ceiling. There was silence in the room with 12 hungry souls seeing their dinner vanish. Poor NK and team had to start from scratch and cook dinner all over again. Clearly, Murphy's Law was at play. Krish attended to some minor medical complaints in the group.

Day 2 started with usual morning tea and breakfast. The trekkers were tired from exertions of the previous day. The trek to Ishtahari was 13 km, a mix of steep climb followed by plain terrain. The team walked alongside the dry riverbed. The progress was slow and the group reached Ishtahari in the evening. The complaints about muscular pain and blisters were getting louder. The medicine man Krish was fighting a losing battle. The team had early dinner and slept to ensure they were ready for a long trek of 18 km next day. Next morning, the group started early. Some of the freshers made slow progress. It was quite clear that this was going

Happy group at Ishtahari

Absorbing sun to recoup

to be a long day. Since I was the last to leave the camp, I had to speed up to ensure I reached the destination ahead of others. Lalit had described the location of inspection bungalow at Dharwas to me and I wanted to make sure we didn't miss it. On the way, Sunil almost lost his sleeping bag which slipped out of his rucksack and rolled down the slope.

It took some time to retrieve it. I took a tumble while trying to avoid a herd of mules on the trail. The team was eager to reach Dharwas before darkness. We just about made it in time.

The mood in the group after 3 tough days of trekking was a bit gloomy. However, I was not prepared for what was to confront me next morning.

Leader's Dilemma: Middle of Nowhere

Woke up next morning with loud complaints from freshers. They were suffering from stiff muscles and blisters. I was happy to delay the departure since distance to Killar was short (9 km). The team could afford some more rest. This would not satisfy them. They wanted to explore the option of abandoning the expedition and going back to Kishtwar (3 days) rather than complete the trek over the next 5 days. The experienced group and a few others were not in agreement. They wouldn't hear of going back. A discussion didn't throw up a solution. Clearly, I had to find a solution.

I asked the experienced group to leave for Killar and decided to stay back with the freshers along with Sandeep (Deputy Leader). We made some more Maltova and started discussing options. I offered the group a solution which envisaged hiring mules to take them back to Atholi from where they could catch a bus to Kishtwar enroute to Delhi. I indicated to them that the rest of the group will go ahead and complete the trek. I then left them so that they could discuss it amongst themselves.

They deliberated the issue for an hour. Finally, they decided to stay the course. They were willing to face the adversity instead of admitting defeat. The group packed up and started walking towards Killar.

> *"Leaders have to listen to the team.
> Empathy is an important virtue."*

It's a lesson which I learnt for my entire life. I had not been listening to their complaints, consumed in my own world. The team had three tough days of trekking. Some of them, especially the freshers were complaining about aches and pains.

> *"The bigger challenge for the mountaineers is not conquering the peak, it is conquering ourselves."*

Krish crossing the wooden bridge

Chatting at Brindabani

As the group trekked towards Killar, I pondered over the events of the last 48 hours. It was quite clear to me that I must leverage this incident to bring the team together. My job was made easier when we were greeted with big cheer by the group which had left earlier. They were delighted to see all the members. Sunil and Raghu went to the village shop to pick up fresh vegetables. NK and his team made some salad and mixed vegetable for dinner. The mood was quite

Smiling Raghu

upbeat. Krish and Sanjay entertained everyone with some Kishore Kumar numbers. The odds in favour of success of the expedition had improved drastically.

The team gathered tremendous momentum. Every evening next day's plan was discussed. The 16 km trek to Brindabani was tough but the team took it well. They took breaks on the way and being together helped everyone cope with adversity.

Sunil and Sunder resting on the rock enjoying the rapids

Stay at Brindabani was comfortable. The stream nearby was quite soothing. We were now very close to our ultimate destination of Sach Pass.

Next day, we trekked 9 km to Dunai, very close to Sach Pass. As we climbed, the landscape changed and vegetation gave

FMS Expedition 3   53

The rare opportunity for a wash

way to barren rocky terrain. The team stayed in an emergency shelter situated under a huge overhanging cliff giving protection from winter snowfall. We prepared for an early start the next day. We had early dinner, prepared packed lunch and got into the sleeping bags.

Lazing around in a scenic place

Sunder enjoying the 'most beautiful place on earth'

Lazing in the Sun enroute to Dunai

Dangerous approach to the Dunai huts

The Success: Trek to Sach and Beyond

The Dunai huts where the team spent the night before the trek to Sach Pass

It was expected to be a long day since the team had to cover a 15 km trek over the Sach Pass on the other side to Satrundi in Himachal Pradesh. We started at 4 am in darkness with light from torches showing us the way. The trekkers set a steady pace since we had to stay together. After climbing for a couple of hours, the group reached the icy glacier with crevasses. This was a dangerous stretch with new crevasses opening up suddenly. Safety of the group was important. The team made slow and steady progress. It was lighting up when we finally reached the Sach Pass. We spent some time taking pictures.

It was important to move quickly and get to the comfort of Satrundi at a lower level. The weather at the Pass was quite uncertain. The success of the expedition was not only reaching the destination but also making sure all the members got back safely. I was especially concerned about the freshers who were now quite tired after a hard climb and were beginning to slow down. The team reached Satrundi well in time for a hot cup of Maltova preceding our dinner. Everyone was happy and relieved. The celebrations were left for later.

Next day's trek to Tarella, the nearest bus head was 16 km long on a flat terrain. The greenery gradually reappeared. It was a beautiful landscape. The team made good progress. The objective was to catch a local bus to Chamba via Tissa. There was enough time for some lunch before boarding the bus for a 6 hour ride to Chamba, a popular tourist destination. The group reached Chamba late in the evening and checked into Govt. Rest House. It had been a long and tiring day.

Barren mountains with few trees

The boys were longing for Parathas, a wish fulfilled next morning. Everyone was famished having lived on Dal Chawal and Aloo Puri for over a week. The team members had lost weight. We went for local sightseeing before taking a bus to Dalhousie, a popular hill resort. The celebration was planned for the evening. It was time for goodies. We ordered food from outside and gave a break to NK and the team. The evening was memorable, demonstrated by the cheerful mood and camaraderie. Krish and Sanjay were in their elements. There was a lot of friendly banter. Next day, we boarded the bus to Khajjiar known for its green meadows. We spent the day enjoying beauty of the place. Everyone was feeling good. It had been over 10 days since the team had left Delhi. It was time to get back.

The return journey on the train gave the weary trekkers time to relax before getting to the routine at FMS. The successful team was received by the Dean Prof Neelamegham, Lalit and other members of the faculty.

Memories of Expedition 3

The beginning—Lalit with the team at FMS

The cheerful team at the Jammu Railway Station on way to Kishtwar

Pangi Valley

Photo credit: Ashok Dilwali

Mallya crossing the bridge

Bending forward to move ahead; Krish, Uday and Sunder

FMS Expedition 3 63

A hard climb in a difficult terrain

Trek on a trail cutting across Sach Pass

On the glacier near Sach Pass—a dangerous place

Finally, at Sach Pass; Time to smile

FMS Expedition 3 65

The team photo on the trek.
Front (L to R)—NK, Krish, Sanjay, Raghu
Back (L to R)—Sandeep, Uday, Sunder, Sunil, Brandy, Shekar, Hamid

The feeling of success after the hard grind

Leisure time at the scenic meadows of Khajiar

Celebrating success in Khajiar

On our return to FMS after successful Expedition 3. With Dean Prof Neelamegham, Dr Lalit Johri and faculty members Dr Narag and Dr Abdul Aziz

Expedition 2 and 3: Life Lessons Learnt

We encountered difficult situations on FMS Expedition 2 and FMS Expedition 3. From evacuating a sick team member to a situation where half the group wanted to return to the base camp after 3 gruelling days of trekking with the other half wanting to go forward and complete the trek, we saw it all. There were no easy solutions but we collectively ensured we found the right one. The following lessons which I learnt helped me navigate difficult situations in my professional and personal life.

1. Articulating a compelling vision that inspires others to follow.
2. Take appropriate well-reasoned risks.
3. Foster trust and bounded optimism in crisis.
4. Teamwork is a force multiplier.
5. Demonstrate perseverance and resilience in pursuit of goals.
6. Empathy is an important virtue.
7. Self-confidence is contagious.
8. Encourage the heart and celebrate success.
9. Confront and resolve tough issues.
10. Play to Win.

Life Lesson 1

Articulating a Compelling Vision that Inspires Others to Follow

"Leadership appears to be the art of getting others to want to do something that you are convinced should be done."

—Vance Packard,
The Pyramid Climbers

Every organization, every social movement begins with a dream. A dream or vision is the force that invents the future. Some call it a vision, others describe it as a purpose, mission, goal or personal agenda. It reflects a desire to make something happen, to change the way things are.

Visions seen only by the leader are insufficient to create an organized movement or significant change. A person with no followers is not a leader, and people will not become followers until they accept the vision as their own. You cannot command commitment, you can only inspire it. Leaders inspire a shared vision. They breathe life into what are the hopes and dreams of others and enable them to see the exciting possibilities that the future holds.

To enlist the people in a vision, a leader must know the followers and speak their language. Leaders communicate their passion through vivid language and expressive style. The leader's own belief in and enthusiasm for the vision are the spark that ignites the flame of inspiration.

Steve Jobs, the enigmatic founder of Apple had a vision of developing 'insanely great products'. It helped him disrupt

Expedition 2 and 3: Life Lessons Learnt   69

computing, music, telephony and retail industries. He believed that the customers must fall in love with Apple products. His vision continues to inspire Apple today.

'Simplicity is the ultimate sophistication' enabled Apple to focus on minute details important from the customer perspective and develop great products. The customer was involved in the entire development process. Today, it's a $ 2 tn company.

Defining the business around its customers and not its products or competitors has helped Amazon evolve from an online bookseller to a retail and an entertainment giant.

Every activity has to have a purpose. It is imperative for a leader to articulate that and ensure that there is a clear buy in from the team. He may choose to consult critical members of his team while arriving at the vision. What is true in corporate life is also relevant in an expedition situation.

In retrospect, I should have invested more time and effort in discussing the purpose and direction before we embarked on the trek. I have always wondered why people climb mountains or go on difficult treks. My reason for participating in the trekking expeditions was my love for the mountains. Overcoming the challenges always adds to your confidence. It also teaches you humility. The vision for the treks was never articulated and looking back, it should have been. All of us had reasons for being there. Some wanted to test their endurance, some joined to seek excitement in adventure, self-confidence and pride.

I spent time in working out the nitty gritty before and during the trek. While this was important, I missed the more important part of engaging with the team and making them stakeholders in the success of the expedition. Leaders have to continuously communicate with the organizations they lead not only to ensure alignment and performance but also raise the level of passion and excitement around shared goals. Missions and projects are successful only when there is a well-oiled team with deep bonds and trust and a shared goal.

Life Lesson 2

Take Appropriate, Well-Reasoned Risks

"I learned that courage was not the absence of fear, but the triumph over it. The brave man is not he who does not feel afraid, but he who conquers that fear."

—Nelson Mandela

Leaders are pioneers—people who are willing to step out into the unknown. They are people who are willing to take risks. They are likely to make mistakes going down the path not trodden before. They will encounter some failures along the way. You should be brave enough to fail as a leader. Many important lessons are learned from failures. Leaders are learners. They learn from their mistakes and their successes.

Risk is inherent in every venture. There is no simple test to predict risk on mountains accurately. We must weigh costs and benefits, potential losses versus gains. For a manager who leads a failed project, it could be a stalled career or a loss of job. For an entrepreneur, it could be loss of personal assets. For a mountain climber or a trekker, lives are at risk. There were so many failed expeditions on Mount Everest and many lives were lost before Tenzing and Hillary made it in 1953. We must factor in the present skills and determination of the team members and the demands of the task.

The trek had difficult stretches where the risks were not very apparent. There were hidden risks of falling stones, sudden change in weather, flash floods and poisonous flora and fauna. It was only on the morning of the day we crossed Sach Pass that we confronted real danger in the form of crevasses on the glacier. We minimized the risk by crossing this part before sunrise. Needless to say, there is no zero risk option when you are in wilderness.

Many important lessons are learned from failures. While it is tempting to let the past memories fade, the lessons are too precious to go unrecorded.

Bill Gates has famously said "It's fine to celebrate success but it is more important to heed the lessons of failure".

Any expedition like starting a new enterprise is a risky business. There are dangers lurking at every turn. A wrong move can be fatal. Looking back, I can say that some well-reasoned risks were taken along the way. Clearly, the ego has to take a back seat when it comes to the overall well-being of the team. Big mountaineering disasters have taken place due to the egos of the participants. Same applies to corporate life.

Life Lesson 3

Foster Trust and Bounded Optimism in Crisis

*"We are now in this war. We are all in it—all the way...
We must share together the good news and bad news, the
defeats and the victories. So far, the news has all been bad."*
—President Franklin D. Roosevelt
(December 1941)

In the time of crisis, it's critical for a leader to build trust within the team. Leaders who build trusting relationships within their team feel comfortable with the group. They are willing to consider alternative viewpoints and to utilize other people's expertise and abilities. While substantial levels of trust may not be required in routine situations, trust is almost always needed when leaders are accomplishing extraordinary things especially in crisis situations. Honesty and candor go a long way in fostering trust. In addition, a reasoned optimism about the future would give confidence and hope to the team.

The past experience of the leader and detailed information and planning of the venture lends credibility to the leader. Also, a sense of humour and lighthearted conduct in stressful situations can dissipate the stress and foster trust. On a trek, decisions have to be taken in real time depending on the situation. Discussions within the team go a long way in building trusting relationships and environment.

Leaders must find an inner calm during the storm. The ability to detach from the crisis and think clearly is absolutely critical. In a crisis, the job of the leader is to navigate point to point. Need to define the required action with a short-term horizon keeping the ultimate mission in mind. This navigation requires tolerance for ambiguity and a possibility of a failure. Evaluating progress against short-term goal can add confidence to the team.

Sitting with the team in Dharwas, in midst of a crisis, the short-term objective was to get to the next stop, Killar, a district headquarter town which was only 9 km away. The ultimate objective to cross Sach Pass seemed quite distant.

I called for a meeting with both the groups to discuss all the possible scenarios with them. There was a group which wanted to move forward and the other group though smaller in size wanted to return. We had a transparent and candid dialogue between the two groups. Finally, told the group which wanted to move forward to go ahead and wait at the next halt Killar. Sandeep and I stayed back with the second group which wanted to return. We sat down to discuss the options over multiple mugs of hot Maltova. Acknowledging the concerns of this group and listening to them itself restored some amount of trust and enthusiasm. The decision to move ahead and not return was taken by the group.

Life Lesson 4

Teamwork is a Force Multiplier

"Teamwork is one of the hallmarks of a good football team— in a team you make each other better."

—Jurgen Klopp,
Liverpool Manager

A team is a tapestry of individuals with different competencies. Leaders who are self-aware and know their strengths and weaknesses can fill their skill gaps with colleagues that complement them. It is for the leader to ensure he gets the best out of every member of the team for the cause of the organization. Leaders understand that they can make greater contribution to the organization if they work with their team than working alone. Progressive companies provide systems and processes that encourage teamwork by recognizing and rewarding both individual and team accomplishments. The system and processes balance the needs and priorities of the company with those of its individual units and functions. This also entails that the employee devotes his energy to fighting competition and not his fellow employees. The company would expect its employees to treat others as they themselves wish to be treated.

In determining the style and power to be used in a given situation, the leader should consider the readiness of the teammates to accept power and authority. Teammates who are used to taking a clear direction may not be ready to adapt to a leader with a consensus style. Conversely, teammates who are highly creative and independent will not respond positively to a directive style. The leader should carefully think about the kind of relationship he wants to have with the team to achieve the goal.

"I get things done by identifying with the people in the company and by trusting them. I care most about building a good team to lead the company" said Anne Mulcahy, Chairperson and CEO of Xerox who turned around the company. Xerox was facing a massive liquidity crisis and was on the verge of bankruptcy. When she was appointed as a CEO, she had no financial experience. She was tutored by the treasurer's office and surrounded herself with diverse set of leaders. She had to build a good team to succeed.

Great teamwork is an essential factor for the success of expeditions, projects or missions. It has a multiplier effect in challenging situations. On both expeditions, we realised that everyone had to contribute if we wanted to succeed. It was heartening to see individuals slip into roles they were comfortable with. Kamal, NK, Navin and Raghu were happy to get involved in cooking. Chandra was an outstanding darner on the trek. Krish was the medicine man on both treks who excelled in this role apart from belting out the songs. Sandeep, Shekar and I would help with bringing buckets of water from the nearest source. Others would help with other chores. This helped enhance the productivity of the team.

On trekking expeditions, teamwork goes beyond sharing of roles and chores. It involves laying solid foundations for collaboration, adoption and maintenance of team norms, boosting team energy and enthusiasm. On both expeditions, this aspect got better as the treks progressed and led to greater bonding in the team.

Life Lesson 5

Demonstrate Perseverance and Resilience in Pursuit of Goals

"The greatest rewards come only from the greatest commitment."

—Arlene Blum,
Leader, American Womens' Himalayan Expedition

Unexpected crisis are an opportunity for resilient leaders to show their mettle. They not only steer the team through a difficult situation but also illuminate opportunities in adversity. Leaders have to demonstrate resilience, an ability to adapt to adversity. Resilient leaders are like shock absorbers.

Uncertainty causes anxiety, self-doubt and fear of failure. It also leads to fear of other's judgement and loss of focus. A certain sense of powerlessness prevails in the environment. The leadership challenge in a crisis is to overcome the bias for inaction. This could be due to lack of information to make the right decision or fear of failure. A leader must also decide what must be done and who will do it. Prioritization, communication and setting the expectation in the short term can go a long way in moving forward.

There are a number of demands on the leader in times of crisis. People want to be heard and they want to be led.

There are situations in crisis when the leader has to demonstrate courage when it's easier to give up. Leaders have to persevere in the face of fear. They have to raise their level of engagement with the team and shift the scale from fear to faith. The leader has to tap into the inner hero.

We faced crisis in both expeditions. A member falling sick on day 1 in a remote location or a small group wanting to go back on day 4 were very unexpected situations. We also encountered challenges every day during the expeditions. There was always an option of turning back. Leaders have to ensure that there is no deviation from the chosen path. Perseverance and resilience are keys to success.

Life Lesson 6

Empathy is an Important Virtue

"Learning to stand in somebody else's shoes, to see through their eyes, that's how peace begins. And it's up to you to make that happen. Empathy is a quality of character that can change the world."

—Barack Obama

Every crisis is unique. There are no off the shelf solutions which can be applied to that situation. It creates an unplanned scenario which leads to uncertainty. In a crisis, a leader when faced with an unprecedented situation can get into denial and can experience a sense of loss of power. Stress, impatience, frustration, apathy and fear are overriding emotions. This triggers anxiety and defensive responses like self-doubt, fear of failure, fear of others' judgement and lack of focus.

The leader can bring about change in the situation which can lead to hope, enthusiasm, high energy and renewed sense of commitment. Empathy, which is an understanding or feeling what another person is experiencing from within their frame of reference is a priceless virtue. Simply put, it is the ability to imagine how the other person is feeling. The leader would need to offer the emotional understanding to his team.

During a crisis, the decision making of the leader can be impaired by the fear of failure and inadequate information to make an informed decision. To navigate through the crisis, a faulty map is better than no map at all. The leader would need to prioritize amongst conflicting demands, communicate immediately and clearly to his team and set short term goals and monitor progress.

This was a huge learning from the Dharwas incident. I was too task oriented, focused on daily 'things to do'. As a leader, I had somehow ignored some members of the team, especially the freshers. They were complaining about issues—real and imaginary. I should have dealt with them earlier on and not allowed the situation to blow up in Dharwas. The balance between task and emotion needed correction.

Empathy for team members has to be reflected in the daily interaction of the leader with them. Bringing a mug of hot beverage for a tired member who needs it or sharing someone's load on the trail demonstrates this behavior. The leader has to understand how each member is feeling to ensure the success of the expeditions. Absence of empathy for individual members can lead to failures with tragic consequences. The history of mountaineering is replete with such examples.

Life Lesson 7

Self-Confidence is Contagious

"I think we all strive to push ourselves, to overcome our struggles. And when we do, we get to know ourselves better."

—Ann Bancroft,
American Explorer

When leaders know themselves well, they become comfortable in their own skin. Without self-awareness, it is easy to get caught up in chasing external symbols of success rather than a person you want to be. It is difficult to regulate your emotions, control your fears, and avoid impulsive outbursts when you feel threatened or rejected. Without being aware of your vulnerabilities, fears and longings, it is hard to empathize with others who are experiencing similar feelings.

Many leaders, especially those early in their careers, are trying to establish themselves in this world that they leave little time for self-exploration. Nor do they focus on being more self-aware. As they age, they may find something is missing in their lives or realize something is holding them back from being the person they want to be. They then drive extremely hard to achieve success in the tangible ways that are recognized in the external world—money, fame, power, status or a rising stock price. Often their drive enables them to be successful, at least for a while, but it may leave them highly vulnerable to being derailed, as their lack of self-awareness can lead to major mistakes and errors in judgement. One of the most difficult things in becoming self-aware is seeing ourselves as others see us. It is self-awareness which helps the leader find real self-confidence. Leader's self-confidence is contagious and can uplift the enthusiasm of the whole team.

As the expedition progressed, the self-confidence and enthusiasm improved. We all go through periods of self-doubt. In such situations, self-belief is what gets you over the hump. One person can uplift the enthusiasm of the whole team. Sandeep's war cry 'Kahan Laake Maara Re' during difficult stretches was indeed uplifting. The key is to take one step at a time. The 3 Cs—Caution, Courage and Camaraderie can foster the 'I can do it' attitude.

Life Lesson 8

Encourage the Heart and Celebrate Success

"For a player—and for any human being—there is nothing better than hearing 'well done'. Those are the two best words ever invented in sports. You don't need to use superlatives."

—Sir Alex Ferguson,
Manager, Manchester United Football Club

Getting extraordinary things done in an organization is hard work. The climb to the summit is arduous and steep. The leaders inspire others with courage and hope. Cheerleading is a large part of the leader's function. Leaders can't get extraordinary things done without teams. Encouraging the heart is not only the process of recognizing individual achievements but also includes celebrating the efforts of the entire group.

Cheerleading and celebrating are the processes of honoring people and sharing with them the sweet taste of success. On a difficult project, planning small wins along the way can motivate the team and help them raise their level of performance. For this to work, the leader must keep his ear to the ground to understand how the members of the team are feeling about the progress.

On tough treks, the breaks in between and a casual chat over a cup of hot beverage can raise the level of energy in the group. This was done very successfully in Expedition 2. In fact, once we stopped to have a quick refreshing shower under a waterfall. This proved to be highly invigorating.

In both FMS Expedition 2 and 3, success was celebrated at the end in Srinagar and Dalhousie respectively. After the hard trek, we had an evening of fun and frolic to unwind and relax. Needless to say, the special evening in Killar during Expedition 3 turned the mood in the group.

The famous mountaineer Mallory when asked why he wanted to climb Everest said "Because it is there". Apart from facing up to challenge, it also underscores the pride which mountaineers experience after successful expeditions. Celebrating success with the team will ensure long term benefits including promoting better bonding and teamwork. The celebratory evenings in Srinagar and Dalhousie will stay in our memories for life.

Life Lesson 9

Confront and Resolve Tough Issues

"There is no worse mistake in public leadership than to hold out false hopes soon to be swept away."
—Winston S. Churchill

In professional and personal lives, we are bound to encounter tough situations. There is a tendency to kick the can down the road. However, in a crisis, leaders need to confront and resolve tough challenges. In both expeditions, we encountered tough situations. In Ikhala (Day 2) during Expedition 2, the situation required quick and practical actions; Dharwas (Day 4) situation during Expedition 3 required quick and satisfactory resolution.

When these situations do arise, you need to inquire (ask) first and then advocate (tell). The leader needs to understand what's going on, the causal factors for the problem. The emotions are normally elevated in these situations so it's important to get them understood and calmed as quickly as possible through a level headed approach. We lose some rationality when we are 'hot' and allow emotions to rule the day.

The leader needs to recognize the emotions of the moment, his and the team's. He needs to ask how others are feeling and listen. Everyone should know why it is important to resolve the issue. In these situations, the leader has to feel the pulse by using listening skills to truly understand other

86   *Beyond the Mountains: Overcoming the Challenges Within*

person's point of view. Asking open ended questions is an imperative to bring out the critical information. The leader would need to share his perspective, without blaming other person/s. Over a period of time, leaders develop a sixth sense which helps them feel the emotional well-being of the team.

It is important to work together on a positive plan of action to resolve the situation by demonstrating flexibility and continuous adaptation. Make a plan together and identify the next logical step in the plan. Do appreciate the other persons' efforts and thank them for helping you resolve the situation.

Planning session for the task ahead

Expedition 2 and 3: Life Lessons Learnt 87

Both Lalit and I faced tough situations early on in the trek. Lalit faced it on Day 2 in Ikhala and I faced a split group in Dharwas. There was no walking away from these. The situations had to be resolved. I had to listen to both the groups and find a way forward. Decisive action and well-reasoned risks acceptable to all had to be taken to ensure success.

Leaders often play on the power of doubt and judgement in such situations. The role of confidantes cannot be under-estimated. Lalit could always depend on me during Expedition 2 and I had Sandeep to back me up in Expedition 3. It was also important to restore the confidence of the small group which wanted to return. A short trek from Dharwas to Killar which the group completed without any problem also helped.

Life Lesson 10

Play to Win

"I hate to lose more than I love to win."
—Jimmy Connors

The big challenge which the leader faces during crisis is balancing defense and offense. There are two competing mindsets.

	Playing Defense	**Playing Offense**
Attitude	Improvement, Efficiency, Execution	Risk-taking, Creativity, Experimentation
Goal	Doing what we know better	Discovering what we don't know
Ethos	Subtraction mindset	Addition mindset

Playing defense and offense simultaneously is a difficult task. During crisis, the leaders have a choice to make. Every crisis throws up opportunities since most of the competition is retreating. Most leaders are playing 'Not to lose'. This is characterized by defensive, passive, reactive and self-limiting behavior. The fear of pain from losing is greater than the pleasure from winning. 'Playing to win' entails relentlessly pursuing new opportunities with a single-minded commitment to winning. This drives a behavior which is offensive, assertive, proactive and solution oriented.

Expedition 2 and 3: Life Lessons Learnt 89

The success of FMS Expedition 2 and 3 is a testimony to the 'Playing to win' approach. In both cases there was a crisis to be addressed. When it would have been easier to follow 'Not to lose' option, the leaders decided to 'Play to Win'.

The day when Lalit and I were taking Dalip back to Palmar will stay with me for life. Lalit, the leader had taken the difficult decision of sending him back. Dalip was not in good shape. In fact, he lay down on the rock and refused to move. We had to take some risks to ensure his safety. We persuaded him to walk to a nearby dhaba in order to find a solution to the problem. Lalit asked me to trek to Palmar to consult a doctor and get the appropriate medicine for Dalip while he kept him company. I returned with medicine in the evening. We decided to spend the night in the small dhaba. After a restful night and the medicine, Dalip felt better the next day. We took him on a mule to Palmar and put him on a bus to Kishtwar for onward journey back to Delhi.

In trekking and mountaineering, the binary choice—offense and defense doesn't work. You have to combine both seamlessly. As per the Chinese war philosophy, offense and defense are two sides of the same coin. Against insurmountable risks, you have to wait, watch and prepare; when you sense or create opportunity, then you have to move.

The Big Lessons for Life

"Life's a bit like mountaineering-never look down."
—Edmund Hillary

Understanding the Stockdale Paradox

The leader must never confuse faith that you will prevail in the end—which you can never afford to lose—with the discipline to confront the most brutal facts of your current reality, whatever they may be. Witnessing this philosophy of duality, author Jim Collins went on to describe it as Stockdale Paradox.

The name refers to Admiral Jim Stockdale, who was the highest-ranking military officer in the 'Hanoi Hilton' POW camp during the height of Vietnam War. Tortured over 20 times during his 8 year imprisonment from 1965-73, Stockdale lived out the war without any prisoner's rights, no set release date, and no certainty as to whether he would survive to see his family again. He shouldered the burden of command doing everything he could to create conditions that would increase the number of prisoners who would survive unbroken.

During an interview with Stockdale by Jim Collins, "I never lost faith in the end of the story, I never doubted not only that I would get out, but also that I would prevail in the end and turn the experience into the defining event of my life, which in retrospect I will not trade", said Stockdale.

On being asked the question "Who didn't make it out?" He said "The optimists, the ones who said we are going to be out by Christmas, we are going to be out by Easter and then we are going to be out by Thanksgiving, they died of a broken heart."

The first big lesson for life I have learnt from these experiences is—

'The most effective leaders in crisis are brutally honest about the situation (Facts). They offer a rational basis for optimism (Hope) and an emotional understanding for their teams (Empathy). Needless to say, honesty and candor promotes trust and reasoned optimism about the future gives confidence and hope.'

In 2020, the world has undergone massive transformation due to Covid crisis. Unlike the financial crisis in 2008-09, this crisis has multiple dimensions. There are humanitarian and economic dimensions apart from the medical dimension. It has hit most countries and most industries simultaneously. This has pushed leaders and organizations beyond existing capabilities, resources and knowledge. This calls for resilient leadership.

This crisis also gives opportunities to the emerging young leaders to think out of the box. In developing economies like India, the poor and marginalized have suffered disproportionately.

'Empathy' is a priceless virtue in such situations. This is the 'mantra' which the younger generation needs to imbibe if they aspire to lead in the future.

Final Take

Now, with the benefit of hindsight, I would like to say that being on Expedition 2 and 3 was only the beginning of a journey of personal transformation. The subsequent 35 years corporate career only reinforced what I learnt during that phase. Every new crisis only adds to the learning.

The world is changing at an accelerated pace. The digital economy is experiencing exponential growth. We are witnessing a new generation of digital operating models transforming the economics and nature of service delivery. The Covid crisis has been a catalyst for change. While technology is facilitating the change, the leaders are still in the driving seat. Companies are leveraging Artificial Intelligence (AI) to scale up operations and gain the competitive edge through speedy service and increase in productivity. This requires different skill-sets and acquisition of tools to keep pace. We would need to reinvent ourselves once again. It is quite clear that the journey of transformation doesn't end. It is a continuous process of evolution.

Finally, no matter how much ever you may be overwhelmed by the technology, there is no better way to train as a leader than to participate in the next available opportunity to join a trekking or mountaineering expedition. The mix of collective enthusiasm, energy and actions is priceless without which neither Lalit or I would have achieved success. It was team success all the way!

I have been through various ups and downs in my career. The biggest lesson of life learnt through my experiences has been—

> *"During the journey of life, when you encounter troughs and peaks, it is important to demonstrate reasoned optimism and courage during troughs and moderation and humility at peaks. The behavior during troughs determines how fast you come out of it".*

Bibliography

1. The Leadership Challenge: How to Get Extraordinary Things Done in Organizations by James M. Kouzes and Barry Z. Posner.
2. Lead Like It Matters: Because it Does by Roxi Bahar Hewertson.
3. Sessions on 'Leading in Adversity' and 'Playing to Win' by Prof. Ranjay Gulati, HBS.
4. Sessions on 'Crisis Management for Leaders' by HBS Faculty.
5. Good to Great: Why Some Companies Make the Leap... Others Don't by Jim C. Collins.

A Leader

I went on a search to become a leader.

I searched high and low. I spoke with authority; people listened but, alas, there was one who was wiser than I and they followed him.

I sought to inspire confidence but the crowd responded, "Why should we trust you?"

I postured and I assumed the look of leadership with a countenance that glowed with confidence and pride. But many passed me by and never noticed my air of elegance.

I ran ahead of the others, pointing the way to new heights. I demonstrated that I knew the route to greatness. And then I looked back and I was alone.

"What shall I do?" I queried. "I've tried hard and used all that I know."

And I sat me down and I pondered long.

And then I listened to the voices around me. And I heard what the group was trying to accomplish.

I rolled up my sleeves and joined in the work.

As we worked I asked, "Are we all together in what we want to do and how to get the job done?"

And we thought together and we fought together and we struggled towards our goal.

I found myself encouraging the faint-hearted. I sought the ideas of those too shy to speak out.

I taught those who had little skill. I praised those who worked hard.

When our task was completed, one of the groups turned to me and said, "This would not have been done but for your leadership."

At first I said, "I didn't lead, I just worked with the rest."

And then I understood, leadership is not a goal. It's a way of reaching a goal.

I lead best when I help others to go where we've decided we want to go.

I lead best when I help others to use themselves creatively.

I lead best when I forget about myself as leader and focus on my group, their needs and their goals.

To lead is to serve. To give to achieve TOGETHER.

Kathryn Nelson
National Leadership Conference